LEARNING TO LIVE SERIES

LIVING
IN THE WORLD

A MINISTRY OF THE NAVIGATORS
P.O. Box 6000, Colorado Springs, Colorado 80934

The Navigators is an international Christian organization. Jesus Christ gave His followers the Great Commission to go and make disciples (Matthew 28:19). The aim of The Navigators is to help fulfill that commission by multiplying laborers for Christ in every nation.

NavPress is the publishing ministry of The Navigators. NavPress publications are tools to help Christians grow. Although publications alone cannot make disciples or change lives, they can help believers learn biblical discipleship, and apply what they learn to their lives and ministries.

© 1987 The Navigators Great Britain
All rights reserved, including translation
ISBN: 0-89109-058-4
10587

Printed in the United States of America

Contents

Author

The LEARNING TO LIVE series was written by Peter Dowse. Born in Great Britain, he has degrees from Cambridge University and London Bible College. Peter has been on staff with The Navigators since 1977. He led the student ministry at Sheffield University for several years, and now gives his time to writing and speaking.

Make the Most of This Bible Study

We live in a world of shifting values and conflicting viewpoints. Is it possible in the midst of this to know what is right and what is true? Yes it is! For God is true, and He has chosen to give us in the Bible a definitive expression of His own mind and will, His knowledge of reality, and His thoughts and plans for the world.

You will know the truth,
and the truth will set you free.
(JOHN 8:32)

It is the aim of this Bible study series to introduce you to the joy and privilege of digging out that truth for yourself.

Personal Bible study is demanding. You will need to give it much time and serious endeavor. In this series, each lesson takes two to three hours to prepare. The rewards of personal Bible study, however, are great. You will surely discover this for yourself as you complete the books in this series.

Remember that Bible study is not merely an academic exercise. You will need to think, but don't forget that the Bible is God's Word. Pray before you start each lesson. Ask God to help you understand the truths and make you sensitive to what He wants to say to you through a particular lesson. Pray as you study, "Lord, what does this mean? How does this relate to

5

me?" Praise Him when you discover something that excites you. The fruit of Bible study should not be just increased head knowledge; it should produce a deeper relationship with God and a lifestyle that is more honoring to Him.

If you can find others who are willing to put in the time to do personal preparation, you will find great value in meeting together to discuss each lesson. But don't let the absence of such a group deter you. Get into God's Word for yourself. You won't be disappointed.

> *When your words came, I ate them;*
> *they were my joy and my heart's delight.*
> (JEREMIAH 15:16)

SOME EXPLANATIONS: The definitions given throughout this series are, of necessity, brief. More exhaustive definitions of the words can be found in any good Bible dictionary, for example, *The Illustrated Bible Dictionary*, published by Inter-Varsity Press.

Whenever the name of a person who has been quoted is followed by an asterisk, you will find information about that person in "Who's Who" on page 97.

Additional references are listed for some questions. They are optional references that you can use if you want to. For an example, see question 8 on page 16.

Each lesson has sections entitled "Ask Yourself." These do not require written responses, though you may want to write answers to the questions in a notebook. Each lesson also has a section entitled "For Further Study." These sections are optional.

The six books in the *Learning to Live* series can be done in any order, or you can follow this suggested sequence:

Clarifying Your Commitment
Living by His Grace
Living in the World
Disciplines of Living
Your Part in His Plan
Standing Firm

Considering the Commandments

In this book, we turn our attention very specifically to lifestyle. The book focuses on the Ten Commandments given by God to the people of Israel at Mount Sinai. One of Satan's devices has been to make people think that keeping these commandments is the key to salvation. Clearly, this is not the case. On the contrary, these standards expose our sin and drive us to seek salvation through faith in Jesus Christ and His work on the cross. Nonetheless, they do reveal God's desire for human behavior. Along with the teaching of the New Testament, they provide us with a way to learn the lifestyle God wants of us.

The first three commandments deal specifically with our relationship with God. You can study those in the book entitled *Standing Firm*. In this book, we will consider the fourth through the tenth commandments.

Work and Rest

The fourth of the Ten Commandments given to Moses states, "Six days you shall labor and do all your work." But is work a necessary evil, or creative service? In this lesson, we will examine what the Bible teaches about work. Interpreting the biblical teaching and applying it in contemporary society are not easy tasks, but they are of utmost relevance to us.

The Fourth Commandment continues, "But the seventh day is a Sabbath to the LORD your God." This is the principal purpose of the commandment—establishing the weekly Sabbath day. It is to be a regular break in the normal cycle of work—a special day, a holy day. This principle of limiting and ordering our work and setting aside special time for God has obvious implications in our hectic society.

Pause for Prayer

Before you begin this lesson, read the entire Fourth Commandment:

Remember the Sabbath day by keeping it holy. Six days you shall labor and do all your work, but the seventh day is a Sabbath to the LORD your God. On it you shall not do any work, neither you, nor your son or daughter, nor your manservant or maidservant, nor your animals, nor the alien within your gates.

For in six days the LORD made the heavens and the earth, the
sea, and all that is in them, but he rested on the seventh day.
Therefore the LORD blessed the Sabbath day and made it holy.
(Exodus 20:8-11)

According to Psalm 119:2, "Blessed are they who keep his [the Lord's] statutes and seek him with all their heart." Before you begin your study, ask God to give you a heart to seek Him and obey Him wholeheartedly in this area of work and rest.

A Working Person

1. Read Genesis 1:26-2:15.

   a. What does this passage tell us about God's nature as it relates to work?

   b. "God created man in his own image" (verse 27). What does this teach us about man and work?

   c. What place did work have in God's original plans for man?

2. Genesis 3 describes man's rebellion against God (the Fall). According to verses 17-19, what effect did this have on man's work?

Since the Fall, work has been marked by frustration. But according to the Bible, we can look forward to a future when we "will not toil in vain" (Isaiah 65:23). And in some measure, as Christians we can enter into God's original purpose here and now; we can use our gifts and abilities to work together with God in the creative management of this world. In doing this, we find fulfillment as human beings. The command to labor was given for our good. This can help explain why unemployment (or some forms of employment) can be demoralizing.

We must not make the mistake of equating work only with paid employment. The housewife engaged in caring for home and family is unpaid, and yet she is clearly doing a most significant work. Students work at learning. Volunteers use their time in creative service to the community. Even those who are paid for their efforts have important work to do above and beyond their jobs.

Working for Money

3. Read the following passages. What are some possible reasons for being employed to earn money?

Matthew 5:13-16

Ephesians 4:28

1 Thessalonians 4:11-12

Additional references: Acts 20:33-35; 1 Timothy 5:8;
Titus 3:14

The Bible demonstrates God's approval of many kinds of occu-
pations. Abraham was a successful herdsman and trader.
Joseph, Esther, and Daniel served in pagan governments. David,
before he became king, was a shepherd and then a musician. In
the New Testament, Luke was a doctor, Paul a tentmaker, and
Lydia—the first Christian in Europe—a businesswoman. Jesus
Himself spent many years working as a carpenter.

Although in the Old Testament priests were set apart specifically for religious services, under the New Covenant sacred/
secular distinctions are abolished. Every Christian is a priest
called into the full-time service of Christ (see Revelation 1:5-6).
Some serve in specific roles within the Church, but the majority
of Christians are called to serve Christ in so-called secular jobs.

---

4. What does 2 Thessalonians 3:6-15 teach about work? (The
   word *idle* refers to people who *will* not work as opposed to
   those who are involuntarily unemployed or engaged in
   work such as looking after home and family.)

Attitudes at Work

5. Unless we run a one-person business, employment involves us in a network of working relationships. The New Testament doesn't directly address the employer-employee relationship of modern society. However, there are some parallels with the master-slave relationship, which the New Testament does deal with. In a limited sense, employees sell themselves—their physical and mental abilities—to their employers. By so doing, they put themselves under authority.

   With this in mind, what can you learn from the following passages about the attitudes you should have as a Christian at work? (All human authority is limited; the illegitimate use of power must be resisted.)

   Colossians 3:22-4:1

   1 Timothy 6:1-2

   Titus 2:9-10

   Additional reference: 1 Peter 2:18

6. Much modern employment falls short of the creative service God intended work to be. So wherever possible, Christians must work to improve deficient working practices and conditions. At the same time, we are called to display Christ-like attitudes in the midst of the real (fallen) world. This may make it necessary at times to submit to less-than-ideal situations.

"I think he's missing the whole point!"

What attitudes are called for in the verses below? How can you apply them in your work?

Philippians 2:3-4

Philippians 2:14-16

7. What can you learn from Jesus' example in John 17:4?

ASK YOURSELF: a. How has my understanding increased concerning the value and purpose of work? b. How can I change my attitudes at work?

For Further Study

Read about the woman pictured in Proverbs 31:10-31. What can you learn from her attitude toward work? In what way do you need to follow her example?

Remember the Sabbath

In Genesis 2:3, we read that God rested from (or ceased) His work of creation on the seventh day. The Hebrew word *Sabbath* comes from the verb "to cease."

8. What can you learn about the purpose of the Old Testament Sabbath from these references?

Exodus 20:8-11

Exodus 34:21

Leviticus 23:3

Isaiah 58:13-14

Additional references in Exodus: 16:1-31; 31:12-17

At its best, the Old Testament Sabbath was very worthwhile. At its worst, it became a mere outward form, and as such was condemned by the prophets (see Isaiah 1:10-17 and Amos 8:4-10). By the time of Jesus, tradition had added numerous petty rules and regulations that precisely defined unacceptable work. Such activities as tying a knot, lighting a fire, moving a lamp, preparing a meal, and even healing, were prohibited.

9. Look at the ways Jesus used the Sabbath. What can you learn from His attitudes?

Luke 4:16

Luke 13:10-17

Luke 14:1-6

The Lord's Day

The first day of the week rapidly replaced the seventh as the customary day for Christians to gather for worship. We find hints of this in Acts 20:7 and 1 Corinthians 16:2. In Revelation 1:10, the day of worship is referred to as "the Lord's Day." Such a designation reflects the fact that Sunday was the day of Jesus' resurrection—the day on which His lordship was revealed beyond question.

For the early Christians, of course, Sunday was an ordinary working day, so they met for worship before dawn. Later it became a day of rest for many.

10. In setting aside a special day, it is important that we have the right attitudes and motivation. What do you find in the passages on page 18 regarding right and wrong attitudes?

Romans 14:5-12

Colossians 2:16-17

"The Sabbath is the golden clasp that binds together the volume of the week." —J.C. MACAULEY

Worship

11. As we have seen, corporate worship was central to the Old Testament Sabbath and the Lord's Day in the early Church. Read the description of heavenly worship in Revelation 5:11-14.

   a. What can you learn from it about the nature of worship?

   b. How can setting aside a special time to worship God help us consecrate our lives to Him?

12. As well as being a time to worship God, the Old Testament Sabbath was also a time for the people to remember that He had made them and redeemed them from slavery in Egypt. What can help you remember to obey the command in 2 Timothy 2:8?

Rest

As we have seen, Jesus had no time for petty regulations regarding the Sabbath. Nevertheless, the Fourth Commandment clearly states the need for a right balance between work and rest. For some, the challenge may be to work harder. Others need to take more seriously the principle of one day's rest in seven.

13. In Exodus 20:10 we read, "You shall not do any work" on the day of rest. What does this mean for you?

In contemporary society, some people must work on Sunday. The early Christians certainly had to do so. If such work is unavoidable, it is important to remember the attitudes we considered in question 10. We can take another day for rest and renewal. And we can find other opportunities to worship with fellow Christians.

14. What principles can you find in the following verses that should influence how you use your free time?

1 Corinthians 6:12

1 Corinthians 10:31

Philippians 4:8

1 Timothy 4:3-5

"The Sabbath was made a day of holy *rest*, so that it might be a day of holy *work*. From this holy work, in our sedentary and lonely world, physical recreation and family fun will not be excluded, but worship and Christian fellowship will come first."[1]
—J.I. Packer

ASK YOURSELF: a. How can I make worship a more central part of my week? b. Does my life reflect the right balance between work and rest? If not, how can I change that?

Stop, Think, and Pray
What have I learned from this study of the Fourth Commandment and other related Bible passages? How has God spoken to me concerning my own life? How do I need to respond?

How God has spoken

How I need to respond

REMEMBER

One way to remember the truths you have studied is to choose key Bible verses and memorize them. You can select your own verses from the passages you study, or memorize the one suggested at the end of each lesson. (See page 95 for help in memorizing Scripture.)

Suggested memory verse about work and rest

Six days you shall labor and do all your work, but the seventh day is a Sabbath to the LORD your God. (Exodus 20:9-10)

==========

NOTES: 1. J.I. Packer, *I Want to Be a Christian* (Wheaton, Illinois: Tyndale House Publishers, 1977), pages 280-281.

Parents and Children

The fifth of the Ten Commandments is the first one to directly address relationships between people. Significantly, it focuses on the family: "Honor your father and your mother."

The family is under great stress in contemporary society. Some see it as an outmoded pattern, a barrier to social progress. Family life, however, is God's idea. It has been a part of His good plan for mankind from the beginning. Yet even those who do not deny the validity of family life find it extremely difficult to make it work without God's guidance and help. The full beauty and joy of life within a family can be discovered only by those who live it God's way.

In this lesson, we will examine the Bible's teaching on one aspect of family life—God's way for parents and children to relate.

Pause for Prayer

The entire Fifth Commandment reads, "Honor your father and your mother, so that you may live long in the land the LORD your God is giving you" (Exodus 20:12). And the writer of Psalm 119:4-5 prayed, "You have laid down precepts that are to be fully obeyed. Oh, that my ways were steadfast in obeying your decrees!"

Ask God to teach you through this lesson, and to give you a

23

desire for full and consistent obedience to the things you learn. The first half of this lesson deals with your relationship as a child to your parents. The second half is a study of your relationship as a parent to your child.

Responsibilities to Parents

Your parents have a unique relationship to you. They gave you life and cared for you when you could not care for yourself. Think about the relationship you currently have with your parents. What is good about it? What is not good about it? How do you feel about it? How do you think they feel about it? Write your thoughts below. (Even if one or both of your parents are now dead, you can still do this.)

Obey

1. Read carefully the two references in the chart on page 23. Then write down in the space provided the content of each command, the reason for the command, and any personal comments you have.

Ephesians 6:1	Colossians 3:20
Command	Command
Reason	Reason
Comments	Comments

In lesson 1, we noted that all human authority has limits (page 13). Parental authority is clearly under the authority of God, so a child who is able to see that his parent's command goes against a clear command of Scripture is justified in disobeying his parent. Larry Christenson writes that such a child "must arm himself with trust in God, not with thoughts of rebellion. He must ask God that He will not permit things to come to such an extremity."[1]

2. There may be a point in life when parental authority ceases to apply.

   a. What ideas in the following passages relate to this issue?

      Matthew 19:4-6

      Mark 3:20-21,31-35

      Luke 2:41-52

   b. What additional factors are important?

   c. What is your conclusion about parental authority?

ASK YOURSELF: To what extent should I currently be living under the authority of my parents?

Honor

Although there may come a point when we are no longer under obligation to *obey* our parents, that must not be allowed to obscure our obligation to *honor* them, which is a lifelong responsibility.

TO HONOR: to hold in respect, to confer distinction upon. Honor is something we owe to our parents simply because they are our parents, regardless of their particular merits or limitations.

---

3. What did Jesus have to say about honoring parents in Matthew 15:1-9?

---

4. What does John 19:25-27 demonstrate about Jesus' commitment to His parents?

ASK YOURSELF: What ideas can I think of to honor my parents?

Love

---

5. What do the passages on page 28 indicate about the priority of family relationships?

Matthew 10:34-39

Matthew 19:28-30

---

6. According to Matthew 22:39, the second greatest commandment is, "Love your neighbor as yourself." Think about what this means for your relationship with your parents.

---

7. The intimacy of family relationships can often test the quality of our love for each other. In the following translation (PH) of 1 Corinthians 13:4-7, underline qualities of love most needed in your relationship with your parents.

This love of which I speak is slow to lose patience—it looks for a way of being constructive. It is not possessive: it is neither anxious to impress nor does it cherish inflated ideas of its own importance.
Love has good manners and does not pursue selfish advantage. It is not touchy. It does not keep account of evil or gloat over the wickedness of other people. On the contrary, it shares the joy of those who live by the truth.

Love knows no limit to its endurance, no end to its trust, no fading of its hope; it can outlast anything.
Love never fails.

ASK YOURSELF: How can I show love to my parents?

---

8. How would you apply the biblical principles considered in the first seven questions to the following situations? (You may identify further information you need, and describe possible solutions for different circumstances.)

SITUATION 1: Dave's parents have recently separated and his father is now living with another woman. Dave's mother wants him to cut off all contact with his father. What should Dave do?

SITUATION 2: Clare has an opportunity to attend an important Christian conference. Her father's birthday is the same weekend, and her mother wants to arrange a family reunion. How can Clare decide what to do?

SITUATION 3: Kevin's mother died recently. His father is elderly and would like Kevin to live with him. What factors should influence Kevin's decision?

SITUATION 4: Judith's parents know that she has been giving money to Christian work. They object strongly and want her to stop. What should she do?

Responsibilities as Parents

If you are not a parent, this section may not have immediate application, and you may prefer to omit the material. However, there is value in seeing what the Bible teaches about this crucial responsibility.

The "Ask Yourself" questions are specially geared to parents. Even though you are not a parent, you may need to change your attitude toward the children you meet. Perhaps you need to be more supportive of friends who are parents. Perhaps the passages have wider relevance than raising children, and can be applied to other relationships. Be creative in your responses.

"Kid's, we're running away from home."

9. Read through Psalms 127 and 128.

    a. How does the psalmist view children?

    b. How should such a view affect the way we behave toward our children?

10. Undergirding all else in our relationship with our children must be that unconditional love that reflects God's commitment to us. Using the Phillips translation of 1 Corinthians 13:4-7 again, underline those qualities of love most relevant to your relationship with your child or children.

This love of which I speak is slow to lose patience—it looks for a way of being constructive. It is not possessive: it is neither anxious to impress nor does it cherish inflated ideas of its own importance.
Love has good manners and does not pursue selfish advantage. It is not touchy. It does not keep account of evil or gloat over the wickedness of other people. On the contrary, it shares the joy of those who live by the truth. Love knows no limit to its endurance, no end to its trust, no fading of its hope; it can outlast anything.
Love never fails.

"The foundation of a solid relationship with our child is unconditional love. Only that type of love relationship can assure a child's growth to his full and total potential. Only this foundation of unconditional love can assure prevention of problems such as feelings of resentment, being unloved, guilt, fear, insecurity. We can be confident that a child is correctly disciplined only if our primary relationship with him is one of unconditional love."[2]

— ROSS CAMPBELL

ASK YOURSELF: In what ways can I convey to my children that I love them unconditionally?

Instruction

11. Consider Deuteronomy 6:4-9 and Psalm 78:5-8. According to these passages, what responsibility does God give to parents?

"I learned more about Christianity from my mother than from all the theologians of England." — JOHN WESLEY*

---

12. Read 1 Thessalonians 2:7-12, in which Paul describes the ministry of his missionary team. What insights do you find about the responsibility of parenthood?

Discipline

"The term 'discipline' is not limited to the context of punishment. . . . Children also need to be taught *self*-discipline and responsible behavior. They need assistance in learning how to face the challenge and obligations of living. They must learn the art of self-control. They should be equipped with the personal strength needed to meet the demands imposed on them by their school, peer group, and later adult responsibilities."[3]

— DR. JAMES DOBSON

13. In the following verses, what guidance about discipline is given to parents?

Ephesians 6:4

Colossians 3:21

In a child's early years, parental control and influence are high. As the child grows, this control should slowly decrease, along with the responsibility for discipline and teaching. However, there should be a corresponding increase in the child's self-control, self-discipline, and learning. (See the diagram on page 35.) The exciting challenge facing parents is to bring up a child who will eventually be a responsible adult.

34

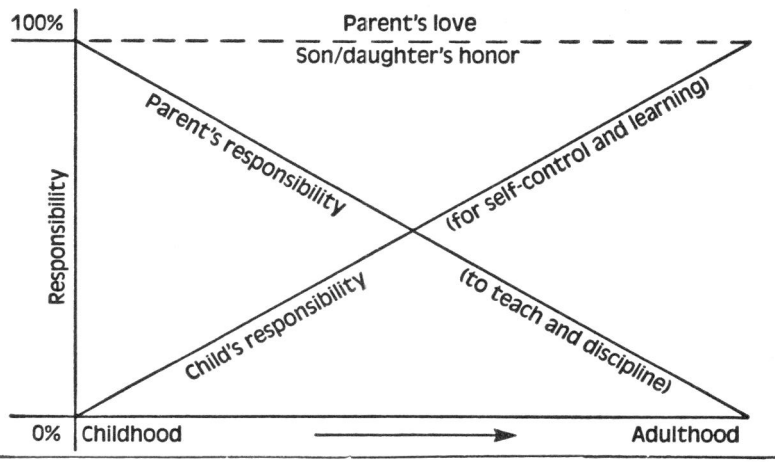

100% ---- Parent's love ----

Son/daughter's honor

Responsibility

Parent's responsibility

Child's responsibility

(for self-control and learning)

(to teach and discipline)

0% | Childhood →→→ Adulthood

14. What does Proverbs 13:24 teach about discipline?

The greatest discipline problem for parents is their self-discipline to establish realistic standards and be consistent in maintaining them. Correction must be fair and controlled, done out of love and in an atmosphere of love.

15. Meditate on the promise in Proverbs 22:6. How do you react to it?

> **ASK YOURSELF:** In what way do I need to change in disciplining my children?

Stop, Think, and Pray

Ask yourself what you have learned about the responsibilities of parents and children. Are you handling your responsibilities well, or has God spoken to you about some needed changes? It may be that He is concerned about a general attitude or kind of behavior.

Put in writing the kind of change you want to see; specify your goal. Then prayerfully think of various activities that might help you reach this goal. Finally, plan a time to review your progress. It's exciting to see God changing you as you faithfully respond to His Word.

REMEMBER

Suggested memory passage about parents and children

> **Children, obey your parents in the Lord, for this is right. "Honor your father and mother"—which is the first commandment with a promise—"that it may go well with you and that you may enjoy long life on the earth." Fathers, do not exasperate your children; instead, bring them up in the training and instruction of the Lord. (Ephesians 6:1-4)**

NOTES: 1. Larry Christenson, *The Christian Family* (Minneapolis: Bethany House Publishers, 1970), page 59.
2. Ross Campbell, *How to Really Love Your Child* (Wheaton, Illinois: Scripture Press/Victor Books, 1977), page 29.
3. James Dobson, *Dare to Discipline* (Wheaton, Illinois: Tyndale House Publishers, 1970), page 13.

Life and Love

Of all ten commandments, the one most universally accepted is the Sixth Commandment: "You shall not murder." It is part of the legal framework of every civilized society. The biblical foundation for the command is the God-given sanctity of human life.

Some Bible translations state the command as, "You shall not kill." This can be misleading, however. The Hebrew word translated as "kill" usually carries the sense of violent killing of a personal enemy. In the Old Testament, the command was not interpreted as prohibiting capital punishment, nor was it regarded as a total ban on war. The Christian response to these issues must also take into account the teaching of the New Testament. Discussion of these issues cannot be resolved by a simple reference to the Sixth Commandment.

Although the command is still accepted, the foundation for it is increasingly being rejected today. This opens the door for more relative estimates of human value and puts at risk the unborn, the sick, the disabled, and the elderly. A consideration of the biblical foundation can help us develop Christian responses to many pressing social issues.

The command has more value, however. The Bible's teaching does not refer only to the outward act of murder. The responsibility to respect the lives of others is in essence an obligation to love them as fellow human beings. Seen in this light, through the perspective of the New Testament, the Sixth Commandment contains something of relevance for each one of us.

Pause for Prayer

Psalm 119:7 reads, "I will praise you with an upright heart as I learn your righteous laws." Before you begin the lesson, take a few moments to praise God for the privilege of having His Word. As you study, ask Him to help you deepen in your understanding and obedience.

The Value of Life

1. Read Genesis 9:1-6.

   a. How does this passage indicate the high value God places on human life?

   b. What reason do you find for this value?

2. The Lord gave Moses some instructions in Numbers 35:9-15. Read the passage.

   a. What did God do about someone who had accidentally killed another person?

b. How does this underline the value God puts on people?

---

3. In addition to idolatry, which sin did the prophets speak about in the following verses?

Jeremiah 19:3-4

Ezekiel 22:1-5

ASK YOURSELF: In what ways is a lack of respect for human life becoming obvious in contemporary society?

For Further Thought

It is no easy matter to work out Christian responses to the many ethical issues confronting contemporary society. The Bible does not directly address many of them, so it is a matter of considering each issue and then searching for relevant biblical principles. In some areas, there is room for Christians to have different opinions.

As an example in biblical thinking, explore an issue such as genetic engineering or euthanasia. If possible, do it as a project with some Christian friends. Below is a suggested approach.
A. Read some books and articles written on the subject.
B. Identify the key biblical principles involved, including relevant passages.
C. As you reflect on these principles and seek to formulate your opinion, consider the conclusions and arguments of

others. It's important to distinguish between those aspects of your conclusion that are clearly required by Scripture and those about which there is room for difference of opinion.

> **ASK YOURSELF:** What can I do to influence society to be more biblical?

"To those who were robbed of life—the unborn, the weak, the sick, the old—during the dark ages of madness, selfishness, lust and greed, for which the last decades of the twentieth century are remembered."[1]

The Debt of Love

The Old Testament does not simply stop after prohibiting killing. It also teaches many other, more positive, things. These are brought into sharp focus in the New Testament.

4. What does Romans 13:8-10 indicate regarding the Sixth Commandment?

5. Read Matthew 5:38-48.

   a. According to Jesus, how should we respond toward an evil person?

b. What should be our attitude toward an enemy?

c. Why should we behave this way?

"To exact an eye for an eye was the accepted norm. But Jesus rejected that way of dealing with evil persons. One should not resist evil in that way. . . . But that does not mean that we cannot offer any form of resistance to the evil person. That would contradict Jesus' own rebuke to the soldier who struck Him on the cheek. Rather it means that Jesus' kind of resistance to evil will be of the sort that refuses to exact equal damages for injury suffered, that refuses to consider anyone an enemy no matter how outrageous his offense and therefore that continues to demonstrate active aggressive love controlled by the need of the evil person. Thus Jesus' saying is compatible with the use of economic, legal or political power to oppose evil as long as love for the oppressor as well as the oppressed is both the means and the end."[2] — RONALD SIDER

---

6. One way we can avoid the command to love people is to label them as enemies. When we categorize people, we are setting them apart from ourselves. We fail to recognize them as equal human beings and succeed in evading our responsibility to love them. But Jesus said, "Love your enemies."

What do you find in the passages below about other forms of discrimination?

Leviticus 19:33-34

James 2:1-9

God's selection of Israel might appear to be discrimination against other nations. However, the Bible indicates that the choice carried no sense of racial superiority (Deuteronomy 7:7-8) and was for the purpose of bringing salvation to all nations (Genesis 12:3). Racial exclusivism in Old Testament history was a necessary practice at times to maintain moral and religious purity (Ezra 9:1,10-12).

"Happy is the man who is able to love all men alike."
— MAXIMUS THE CONFESSOR*

ASK YOURSELF: Am I guilty of valuing people based on their race or education or some other factors? In what way?

Living a Life of Love
It is no surprise to find that love is a recurring theme in the New Testament. However, there are especially meaningful passages. First Corinthians 13 is a lyrical description of the qualities of love. First John is a dynamic presentation of love as the

essential hallmark of a genuine Christian. Virtually every New Testament letter includes practical guidelines on how to demonstrate love in day-to-day life.

For the rest of this lesson, we will focus on Ephesians 4:25-5:2. We will also examine various cross-references in order to deepen our appreciation of the principles. Begin by reading through the passage in Ephesians two or three times.

Motivation, Imitation, Inspiration

7. Read Ephesians 5:1 and 1 John 4:16-5:1. How should God's love for us affect our attitude toward other people?

"If you allow God to share the profound unconditional love He has for you, then it is much easier for you to discover He has the same love for others . . . and we can participate with Him in His . . . love."[3] — E. STANLEY JONES

8. Along with Ephesians 5:2, read Romans 5:6-8 and 1 John 3:16-18. Think about the love God has shown us in Christ. Then write a definition of the kind of love we are to show to others.

9. Focus on Ephesians 4:30.

a. How do we damage our relationship with God?

b. According to Galatians 5:13-26, how does God make it possible for us to live a life of love?

Speech, Attitudes, Action

10. Read Ephesians 4:25 and 29.

a. Describe the kind of speech that is consistent with love.

b. What further insights about speaking with love do you find in these references in Proverbs?

12:18

12:25

15:1

17:9

27:9

27:14

_____

11. Think about Ephesians 4:26-27 and 31-32, along with James 3:14-16 and Romans 12:10 and 15.

   a. What attitudes do we need to guard against?

There is a righteous anger; to be indignant about sin is Christ-like. Such indignation may require a confrontation with another person, but the purpose should always be to help him face his wrong ways and overcome them. The objective should never be to embarrass or hurt.

    b. What attitudes do we need to develop?

---

12. a. What aspect of love do you see in Ephesians 4:28?

    b. What is the basic change of direction indicated by this example? (Also look at Philippians 2:3-4.)

    c. What practical guidance on showing love is found in Matthew 7:12?

ASK YOURSELF: a. How can I deal with unloving attitudes that I have toward certain people? **b.** How can my speech be more loving? **c.** What practical actions can I take to demonstrate love?

Stop, Think, and Pray

What have I learned about the full significance of the Sixth Commandment? How do I need to change in order to respect and love other people more? How has God specifically spoken to me?

How God has spoken to me

What I need to do in response

REMEMBER

Suggested memory verse about life and love

Be imitators of God, therefore, as dearly loved children and live a life of love, just as Christ loved us and gave himself up for us as a fragrant offering and sacrifice to God. (Ephesians 5:1-2)

NOTES: 1. Francis Schaeffer and Everett Koop, *Whatever Happened to the Human Race?* (Old Tappan, New Jersey: Fleming H. Revell Company, 1979), page 5.
2. Ronald Sider, *Christ and Violence* (Scottsdale, Pennsylvania: Herald Press, 1979), pages 42-43.
3. E. Stanley Jones, as quoted in *The Mustard Seed Conspiracy*, by Tom Sine (Waco, Texas: Word, Inc., 1981), page 188.

Man and Woman

God has included within His creation a delightful diversity. Nowhere is this more gloriously seen than in the differentiation of male and female. The creation of the first woman drew from Adam an enthusiasm that was unparalleled in his response to the rest of creation: "This *at last* is bone of my bones and flesh of my flesh" (Genesis 2:23, RSV, italics added). The relationship of Adam and Eve was one of unashamed and joyful harmony. Sadly, the Fall soon shattered their blissful partnership.

The effects of the Fall on all subsequent relationships between men and women are clear for all to see. The most obvious effect is the corruption of the God-given sex drive. Instead of strengthening commitment and unity in an act of self-giving, it has often become a motivating force for cheap and casual acts of self-gratification. The Seventh Commandment addresses this: "You shall not commit adultery" (Exodus 20:14). So, in part, does the Tenth Commandment: "You shall not covet your neighbor's wife" (Exodus 20:17).

The Fall has also introduced unhealthy sexual competitiveness. Instead of recognizing sexual differences and pursuing productive partnerships, the history of the male-female relationship is littered with discord, contempt, and exploitation. The modern feminist movement, in particular, has highlighted the way in which men have often used their power to oppress and demean women. Sometimes this movement has criticized the Bible for its supposed support of male domination.

What does the Bible teach? What effects should sex have on roles and relationships? What is God's pattern for sex and marriage? What about divorce and singleness? We will consider these questions in this lesson.

Pause for Prayer

Along with the author of Psalm 119:18-19, you might pray, "Open my eyes that I may see wonderful things in your law. I am a stranger on earth; do not hide your commands from me." Begin your time of study by expressing to God your utter dependence on Him for true understanding. Ask Him to help you set aside preconceived ideas and to open your eyes to understand His ways.

Equal

1. Read Genesis 1:26-28. What can you discover in these verses about God's attitude toward men and women?

2. According to Genesis 3:16, how does the Fall affect the quality of the relationship between a man and his wife?

Women in Old Testament Israel and New Testament Judaism

Despite a few examples of women holding civil office, life in Israel was male-dominated. The Old Testament marriage laws, criminal codes, and inheritance regulations all assumed the fundamental importance of the family unit. Each one functioned under the legal headship of the senior male, or patriarch. It appears that in the early period the patriarch also acted as the family priest in worship, although under Moses this function was restricted to unblemished male Levites and sons of Aaron.

Nowhere, however, is it indicated that the subordinate legal status of women was based on an assumption of inferiority. On the contrary, the Old Testament offers several examples of women who were wiser and more godly than their husbands. The Old Testament laws also limited the possible abuse of male status and stressed the attendant responsibility to act for the benefit of those under authority.

In the period between the Old and New Testaments (about 400 years), it appears that attitudes toward women in Judaism hardened. They were relegated to a position of inferiority. Jewish men were taught to pray, "Blessed are thou who has not made me a woman!" Although the rabbis praised women for service in the home, they considered them unsuited for public office. Their sexuality and supposed ignorance were held in contempt. Generally, the rabbis did not consider them capable of learning about religious matters; some rabbis actually forbade it. Often women were cited as examples of undesirable traits. Because of the temptation of immorality, segregation was increasingly encouraged.

---

3. What do the following passages in Luke reveal about the way Jesus related to women?

7:36-50

8:1-3

10:38-42

Additional reference: John 4:27

"Although Jesus in no way seeks to deny or diminish the distinction between the sexes—He emphasizes their partnership in marriage—it is nevertheless difficult to find any difference in the approach of Jesus to women and to men. . . . Men and women alike could talk to Jesus, could follow Him, could be friends with Him, could serve Him, could love Him."[1] —MARY EVANS

---

4. What can you learn from the following references about the place in the early Church of both men and women?

Acts 1:13-14, 2:1-4, and 2:17-18

Acts 8:3

Acts 16:13-15

Acts 21:7-9

Romans 16:1-16

Philippians 4:2-3

Additional references: Acts 5:12-14; 8:12; 12:12; 17:4,12,34;
1 Corinthians 11:5; 1 Timothy 3:11; Titus 2:3-5

MY SUMMARY

Complementary

TO COMPLEMENT: to complete, forming a satisfactory or balanced whole.

---

5. Read Genesis 2:18-25. What can you learn from this passage about the relationship between men and women? (The word translated "helper" in verse 18 carries no sense of inferiority. The term is used to describe one who lends a hand or helps out, frequently in a context of need. It is most often used for God in relation to Israel. For an example, see Psalm 70:5.)

---

6. What important truth is brought out in 1 Corinthians 11:11-12?

---

7. Consider the general statement in 1 Corinthians 12:4-7. How do you think this might apply to the way men and women should relate in Christian service?

"On the Day of Pentecost, in fulfillment of prophecy, God poured out his Spirit on 'all flesh,' including 'sons and daughters' and his 'servants, both men and women.' If the gift of the Spirit was bestowed on all believers of both sexes, so were his gifts. . . . We must conclude, therefore, not only that Christ gives [spiritual gifts] (including the teaching gifts) to women, but that alongside his gifts he issues his call to develop and exercise them in his service and in the service of others, for the building up of his body."[2] —JOHN STOTT

ASK YOURSELF: How can I more fully benefit from the complementary natures of men and women?

For Further Study

Three passages in the New Testament make specific reference to men and women in church worship. The passages are interpreted by some as imposing severe restrictions on the role women can play in church life. These passages have been the subject of much debate; the task of interpretation is far from easy. The questions below should help you get into the passages. They do not, however, constitute exhaustive study.

Read 1 Corinthians 11:2-16.
A. What are Paul's instructions concerning the dress of men and women in worship? (In Jewish society, the penalty for adultery was to shave off the woman's hair and expel her from the synagogue.)

B. What could be the background to this teaching? (Two possibilities: a group of women within the church desired to assert their equality in Christ, and so refused to "cover" themselves in worship; the church in general was worried that the custom of women covering themselves contradicted their equality in Christ.)

C. What reasons does Paul give for this instruction?

D. What do you think are the fundamental principles he asserts?

E. How should we apply these principles today?

Read 1 Corinthians 14:34-36.
 F. If this passage requires total silence for women in worship, how can it be reconciled with 1 Corinthians 11:5 and 14:26?

G. If it is not total silence that is required, what particular form of participation is Paul excluding?

H. Is this teaching for all women, including the unmarried, widows, and those with nonChristian husbands?

 I. What underlying principle does this teaching establish?

J. How should we apply this principle?

Read 1 Timothy 2:8-15.

K. Exactly what does Paul prohibit in verse 12? Is it all teaching of men? Is it a particular kind of teaching? Is it wives teaching husbands?

L. What reasons does Paul give for this instruction?

M. What is the fundamental principle underlying this instruction?

N. How should we apply the principle today?

Sex, Marriage, Divorce, and Singleness

Much of Jesus' teaching on sex, marriage, divorce, and singleness is found in Matthew 19:3-12. Read this passage two or three times.

8. In Matthew 19:5, Jesus refers to the experience of sexual intercourse as a man and woman becoming "one flesh." What can you learn about God's attitude toward sex from the passage Jesus quotes (Genesis 2:24-25) and from the other references below?

Genesis 2:24-25

Proverbs 5:18-19

1 Corinthians 7:3-5

Sex is God's gift, not His reluctant concession to man's needs. God created us with the capacity and desire for sexual relationships. The Bible even includes one book, Song of Solomon, that describes the joy of physical lovemaking in marriage. The idea that sex is somehow unChristian is a mark of false teaching. The Bible also emphasizes the importance of the right context for sexual intercourse.

9. Jesus' reference to sex in Matthew 19:5 clearly identifies the context.

a. Based on the following verses, what is the only context in which sex is permissible?

Deuteronomy 22:13-22

Matthew 19:5

Hebrews 13:4

Additional references: Proverbs 5:20-23; Colossians 3:5-8; 1 Thessalonians 4:3-8

"No one can study the teaching of Jesus and of the New Testament without seeing that the teaching stands for purity and chastity. Fornication, which is sexual intercourse between unmarried people, is condemned at least eighteen times. . . . Adultery, which is sexual intercourse with a married person other than one's own marriage partner, is condemned at least fifteen times."[3] — WILLIAM BARCLAY

---

b. Why do you think God restricts sex to marriage?

c. What additional teaching regarding sex do you find in the following passages?

Matthew 5:27-30

Ephesians 5:3-14

"Do not say you have chaste minds if you have unchaste eyes, because an unchaste eye is the messenger of an unchaste heart."
— AUGUSTINE*

Marriage and Divorce

10. In Matthew 19:4-6 Jesus summarizes what is involved in marriage.

a. Based on these verses, write a definition of marriage.

b. In Proverbs 2:17, marriage is described as a covenant made before God. What insight does this give you into the nature of the marriage relationship?

_____

11. In Matthew 19:7-9, Jesus turns to the question of divorce.

a. According to these verses, why did God permit divorce in the Old Testament?

b. Even in the case of marital unfaithfulness, what does Matthew 18:15-27 require of Christians?

c. What further teaching on divorce is given in 1 Corinthians 7:10-15?

d. How does Malachi 2:13-16 describe one of God's purposes in marriage and His attitude toward divorce?

Marriage and Singleness

12. In verses 10-12 of Matthew 19, Jesus talks about singleness.

a. What reason could someone have for not marrying?

b. What additional reasons are found in 1 Corinthians 7:25-28?

c. How does Jesus' teaching in Matthew 22:29-30 affect your view of marriage?

d. According to 1 Corinthians 7:7, both marriage and singleness are gifts from God. How should this shape our attitude toward them?

13. Read 1 Timothy 5:1-2. What can you learn from Paul's instructions to Timothy about the kind of relationships we can enjoy whether or not we are married?

Marriage Relationships

14. In Matthew 19:5-6, Jesus speaks of the unity of man and wife: "They are no longer two, but one."

   a. According to 2 Corinthians 6:14, what implication does this have for Christians in choosing a life partner?

"What a union for two believers is a Christian marriage—to have one hope, one desire, one course of life, one service of God in common one with the other." — TERTULLIAN*

b. Practical unity is not automatic, however, so the Bible gives clear guidelines on how to develop the marriage relationship in such a way as to develop unity. Two key passages are Ephesians 5:21-33 and 1 Peter 3:1-7. Read through these. Then list the respective responsibilities of husband and wife. (Grammatically, Ephesians 5:21 serves both as a conclusion to 5:18-21 and as an introduction to 5:21-6:7. Also, the term *master* in 1 Peter 3:6 did not, in its cultural context, carry the contemporary negative overtones of distance and formality.)

Responsibilities of the husband	Responsibilities of the wife

In studying God's pattern for marriage, it is important to remember Jesus' teaching that a leader must serve. (For example, see Matthew 20:25-28.) The use of authority to dictate and dominate goes directly against biblical teaching.

We must also be wary of reading into biblical teaching our own ideas about tasks that only men or only women should do. The Bible has remarkably little to say on this; our views are usually very dependent on our background.

ASK YOURSELF: a. What have I learned concerning the Bible's attitude toward sex, marriage, divorce, and singleness? **b.** In what ways are my attitudes, actions, and words out of line with biblical standards?

Stop, Think, and Pray

What have I learned from this study? What do I need to remember? Do I need to change my attitude about anything? How are my relationships with those of the opposite sex? What specific things has God spoken to me about, and what response do I need to make?

REMEMBER

Suggested memory verse about man and woman

The LORD God said, "It is not good for the man to be alone. I will make a helper suitable for him." (Genesis 2:18)

NOTES: 1. Mary Evans, *Women in the Bible* (Exeter, England: Paternoster Press, 1983), pages 56-57.
2. John Stott, *Issues Facing Christians Today* (London: Marshall Morgan & Scott, 1984), page 251.
3. William Barclay, *Ethics in a Permissive Society* (Glasgow, Scotland: William Collins Sons & Company Ltd., 1971), page 208.

Honesty and Integrity

"You shall not steal. You shall not give false testimony against your neighbor" (Exodus 20:15-16). These two commandments (the eighth and ninth) establish an essential condition for any society. The Bible, however, goes deeper than mere legal requirements. God desires people who are honest through and through—men and women of complete integrity.

How does this standard compare with the values of contemporary society? We will investigate the biblical teaching and consider its relevance to present-day situations.

Pause for Prayer

The psalmist wrote, "Keep me from deceitful ways; be gracious to me through your law" (Psalm 119:29). Before you begin, thank God that His Word can help you understand where your life is wrong and can direct you more fully in His way.

Understanding Honesty

1. a. Read Psalm 15. What does this psalm reveal about the nature of honesty?

b. What does it teach about the importance of honesty?
Also read Psalm 101:7.

---

2. The words of the Eighth Commandment are clear and familiar: "You shall not steal." The verses below list some ways in which God expects this command to be put into practice. What form of dishonesty is highlighted in each passage? List the way in which you think the teaching of each passage is relevant to your own life.

	Form of dishonesty	Relevance to my life
Deuteronomy 24:14-15		
Deuteronomy 25:13-16		
Romans 13:7-8		

Titus 2:9-10

(You may add other forms of dishonesty that come to mind as you think about the principle, "You shall not steal.")

---

3. As you completed the chart in question 2, you may have recalled dishonest actions in your past. What can you learn from Luke 19:8-10 and 1 John 1:9 regarding your past actions?

(The principle of restitution was built into Old Testament law. See, for example, Exodus 22:1,5 and Numbers 5:5-7.)

---

4. The Ninth Commandment states, "You shall not give false testimony against your neighbor." Specifically, it is dealing with the obligation of a witness in a court of law. In principle, though, it is condemning all untruthfulness.

In each of the references on page 70, what form of dishonest speech is identified? In what way is each verse or passage relevant to your life?

69

Form of dishonest speech	Relevance to my life
Leviticus 5:1	
Jeremiah 23:30-32	
James 4:11-12	
1 Peter 3:10	

(Have other forms of dishonest speech come to mind?)

We may lie because of malice or fear. We may lie for profit, or to show ourselves in a better light. We may lie by remaining silent or telling a half-truth. We may simply become careless about the accuracy of what we say. Speaking the truth always is a difficult discipline, especially if we have had years of practicing falsehood.

5. Consider Matthew 12:33-37. What teaching do you find about the importance of our speech?

6. What does Jeremiah 17:9 teach about the dishonesty within us?

7. What are some ways in which we may even deceive ourselves?

Proverbs 12:11

Romans 12:3

James 1:22

ASK YOURSELF: a. What action can I take to correct past dishonesty? b. What areas of actual or potential dishonesty do I see in my life?

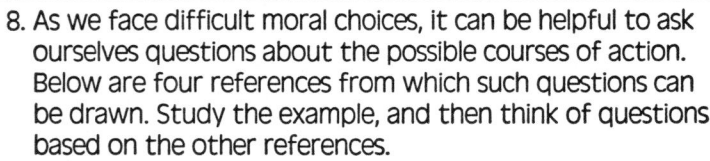

Developing Integrity

Right Decisions

8. As we face difficult moral choices, it can be helpful to ask ourselves questions about the possible courses of action. Below are four references from which such questions can be drawn. Study the example, and then think of questions based on the other references.

John 14:21—Would it mean disobeying a biblical command?

Ephesians 5:8-11

Philippians 1:27

1 John 2:6

9. What important truths does Jesus highlight in Luke 16:10-13?

10. Sometimes your refusal to compromise with dishonesty may involve risk and conflict. How can the principle of Matthew 6:31-34 help you?

A Clear Conscience

11. According to the Apostle Paul, what is the place of conscience in honest living?

Acts 24:16

1 Timothy 1:5-6

1 Timothy 1:18-19

The conscience is a God-given part of our human personality. It is the faculty that morally evaluates our actions, words, thoughts, and motives. However, it is not entirely reliable; like every part of our human nature, it is corrupt because of the Fall. It is also influenced by the wrong standards and values in society.

The Bible speaks of several kinds of conscience:

- A seared conscience (1 Timothy 4:2)—so consistently ignored that it has ceased to function.
- A corrupted conscience (Titus 1:15)—blind to wrong in some areas. The blindness may be a result of conforming to the wrong values of family or society. It may be the result of continued sinful disobedience in a particular area.
- A weak conscience (1 Corinthians 8:7-13)—overly sensitive, attaching moral significance to things God does not.
- A good conscience (1 Timothy 1:5)—in line with God's standards. The expression may also mean "a clear conscience."
- A clear conscience (Acts 24:16)—has been taken into account, resulting in appropriate action. The opposite of a seared conscience.

No one has a perfect conscience. It is often ineffective and unreliable. However, when our conscience speaks, we need to respond to it. The right response is not necessarily to obey immediately. Rather, we should pray about the issue, examine Scripture, and seek Christian counsel. Then we are in a position to decide if our pang of guilt is the result of a genuinely wrong action or the product of faulty thinking.

---

12. God is at work by His Holy Spirit to renew every area of our life, conscience included. How can we cooperate with Him in developing a good conscience?

Psalm 139:23-24

Romans 12:2

Hebrews 3:13

Positive Replacement

13. Meditate on Philippians 4:8. According to this verse, what can we do to control our thoughts?

14. Consider Ephesians 4:22-29.

    a. What is recommended as the alternative to dishonest speech and actions?

    b. Think about the areas in which you are tempted to be dishonest. What can you do or say to exclude wrong thoughts, words, or actions?

"We beseech thee mercifully to shine in our hearts, that the night and darkness of sin, and the mists of error on every side being driven away by the brightness of Thy shining within our hearts, we may all our life walk without stumbling, as in the day time, and being pure and clean from the works of darkness, may abound in all good works which thou has prepared for us to walk in." — ERASMUS*

15. How would you apply principles from the previous questions when advising close Christian friends in the following situations?

    SITUATION 1: Robert was involved in a minor car accident in which a man who had obviously been drinking hit his car. The policeman asked Robert how fast he was going at the time of impact. Robert replied, "About 30 miles per hour, I think" (the speed limit). The following Sunday in church, Robert found himself worrying about his answer. He felt sure that his speed was actually closer to 40 miles per hour.

    SITUATION 2: Sharon lives in a college dormitory. When her friend Naomi comes for a visit, she joins Sharon for a meal in the dining hall. Naomi should buy a guest meal ticket, but since the cost of meals is considered excessive, no one bothers with the system. There is also a rule about guests not being allowed to stay overnight in student rooms, but Sharon lets Naomi do it.

SITUATION 3: Carol is working in a new job. It is the practice every Friday for most of the employees to take an extended lunch break. When Carol joins the group, she doesn't find the conversation very profitable. She finds herself thinking, "Is it right to be here on the company's time?" On the other hand, if she is at the office, she will be virtually alone.

For Further Study

Jacob is an Old Testament character who illustrates the way God works to transform us into people of honesty and integrity. Read about him in Genesis 25:19-34 and 27:1-33:20. How is his dishonesty evident? How does God work to show him the foolishness of it? How does God change him?

Stop, Think, and Pray

What have I learned about God's standards for honesty? Has He exposed areas of dishonesty in my life? What do I need to do to become a person of integrity? What specific actions do I need to take? Should I set some long-term goals?

REMEMBER

Suggested memory verse about honesty and integrity

**No one who practices deceit
will dwell in my house;
no one who speaks falsely
will stand in my presence.
(Psalm 101:7)**

Money and Materialism

The last of the Ten Commandments reads, "You shall not covet your neighbor's house. You shall not covet your neighbor's wife, or his manservant or maidservant, his ox or donkey, or anything that belongs to your neighbor" (Exodus 20:17). This commandment has great relevance for our modern world, in which the acquisition of money has assumed massive importance. Money is desired because it brings power: to influence others; to accumulate material possessions; to attain a more comfortable lifestyle; and to enjoy new experiences.

The Bible has much to say about this love of money. It calls us to a radically different lifestyle in which money and material possessions are put in their proper place. In this lesson we will examine the biblical guidelines on money and its use. The necessity to obey the biblical teaching in this area may prove to be the acid test of our Christian discipleship in our affluent society.

Pause for Prayer

As you begin, pray the words of Psalm 119:36-37: "Turn my heart toward your statutes and not toward selfish gain. Turn my eyes away from worthless things; renew my life according to your word." Thank God that He can give you a true perspective on life. Ask Him to help you gain a fuller understanding of His values as you complete this lesson.

The Ultimate Owner

1. First Chronicles 29:10-20 records what King David prayed after the people of Israel brought gifts for the building of the Temple. From that passage and Psalm 24:1, what can you learn about God and His relationship to material things?

2. Deuteronomy 8:17-18 is part of a warning to the people of Israel as they are about to enter the Promised Land. What important truth do you need to remember?

ASK YOURSELF: If God owns all things, how should this affect my attitude toward my money and possessions?

The Serious Danger

The Bible has a great deal to say about our attitude toward money and material possessions. For many people, the accumulation of wealth and possessions can become a dominating motivation in life.

In this section we will focus on two key New Testament passages: Luke 12 and 1 Timothy 6.

3. Read Luke 12:13-21.

    a. Write verse 15 in your own words.

    b. What is the attitude of the man in the parable that Jesus tells? (Parables are stories that usually have one main point. We should not read significance into every detail in the story.)

    c. Is his attitude right or wrong?

4. Read Luke 12:22-31. Describe the attitude that Jesus wants His disciples to have.

"I fear, wherever riches have increased, the essence of religion has decreased in the same proportion." —JOHN WESLEY*

5. Read Luke 12:32-34.

    a. What do you think Jesus is saying here?

b. What reason does Jesus give for adopting the attitude described in Luke 12:22-31?

"I believe Jesus is asking us to give away what we do not need—such as money, possessions or food—to those who are in need. So let us prayerfully consider these areas. Are we saving for the right purposes, or simply as a prop for our faith? Are we carrying *surplus* possessions which others could use? Are we eating too much?"[1] —JAMES BROAD

---

6. Read 1 Timothy 6:6-10 and 17-19.

a. Based on these verses, along with Proverbs 30:8-9, what can you learn about attitudes toward money?

b. What guidance is given about how to overcome the wrong attitudes? Also read Ecclesiastes 5:10 and Matthew 5:42.

"I bought it because small cars are the spirit of the age."

"The Christian should not accept the capitalist assumption that great abilities or ownership of resources entitles a man to a commensurate level of consumption. . . . Decisions about consumption should start from a consideration of needs, not from the amount of income that there is to be spent."[2] — DONALD HAY

ASK YOURSELF: How can I decide whether or not I have a right attitude toward money and material possessions?

The Responsible Manager

Although materialism is a serious danger, it is not wrong to enjoy the good things God gives us: "God . . . richly provides us with everything for our enjoyment" (1 Timothy 6:17). However, since God is the owner of all things, we must answer to Him for the way we manage the money and possessions He entrusts to us. (Early Bible translations used the word *steward* for a person with delegated responsibility to oversee or manage. Hence, much Christian writing refers to "stewardship.")

---

7. Read Matthew 25:14-30. What does this passage teach about the use of money?

It is important that we don't isolate our management of money from other responsibilities. While it is good to use money to generate more money, this cannot be our only intention. The overriding principle must be the service of our fellow men. To put Matthew 25:14-30 in context, read verses 31-46.

8. Read Luke 16:1-15. This passage includes a parable. Remember that we should not read significance into the incidental details; Jesus is not commending dishonesty!

   a. What quality in the manager is commended?

   b. What importance does Jesus attach to the way we handle money and possessions?

   c. What can you learn from verses 13-15?

9. According to the following verses, what are some ways in which we need to show responsibility in our use of money?

   Proverbs 21:20

   Romans 13:7

   1 Timothy 5:8

Think It Through

An important step in the responsible management of money is knowing where your money is going. List your basic income and regular expenditures for whatever period is most appropriate for you—a week, a month, or a year. The categories listed are suggestions only. (This exercise is also valid for those with unusual patterns of spending, such as students.)

Giving:
Taxes and other deductions:
Housing:
Gas, electricity, etc.:
Telephone:
Food:
Household maintenance:
Car expenses:
Clothes:
Other personal items:
Savings for future needs:
Other:
Other:

At the end of the lesson, you may find it helpful to pray about ways in which to change your spending patterns.

"We lay down no rules or regulations for either ourselves or others. Yet we resolve to renounce waste and oppose extravagance in personal living, clothing and housing, travel and church buildings. We also accept the distinction between necessities and luxuries, creative hobbies and empty status symbols, modesty and vanity, occasional celebrations and normal routine, and between the service of God and slavery to fashion. Where to draw the line requires conscientious thought and decision by us, together with members of our family."[3]

The Generous Giver

As we have seen in several of the passages already considered, money and material possessions can be used in positive ways; for example, to give to those in need. Generous giving reflects God's concern for the poor. It also helps the giver overcome the danger of possessiveness.

In 2 Corinthians 8 and 9, Paul describes the generous giving of the churches in Macedonia, and uses that example to teach the Corinthians about giving. These two chapters contain a useful summary of the biblical principles of giving. Read through them to gain an overview before considering specific details in the questions below.

---

10. Read 2 Corinthians 8:1-15.

    a. What can you learn about giving from the examples of the Macedonians?

    b. What incentive to give is provided by the example of Christ?

    c. What principle is brought out in verses 13-15?

11. What do the following verses teach about the way we should give?

Matthew 6:2-4

1 Corinthians 16:2 and 2 Corinthians 8:10-12

2 Corinthians 9:1-7

"How much should I give?" is a question many Christians ask. In the Old Testament, the people of God were to give a tithe, that is, 10% of a person's income. (See, for example, Leviticus 27:30, Deuteronomy 14:28-29, and Malachi 3:8-18. In fact, a detailed study suggests that the average Israelite must have contributed about a third of his income.)

The New Testament does not emphasize that we should give a particular portion of our income. It stresses that we should give in proportion to what we have for the needs we see. Also, our generosity should be a real cost to ourselves. A tenth may serve as a guide. Above all, make your decision prayerfully.

12. Another important question is, "To whom should I give?" Primarily, your giving is to the Lord and is part of your worship (see Philippians 4:18). Beyond that, what does the Bible teach about to whom your giving should be allocated? Look up the verses listed on page 91 and fill in the chart.

To whom we should give	Specific person or group
Proverbs 19:17	
Luke 12:33	
1 Corinthians 9:13-14	
3 John 5-8	
Galatians 6:6	
1 Timothy 5:17-18	
Matthew 25:34-40	
James 2:15-16	

13. According to 2 Corinthians 9:8-15, what does God promise regarding giving?

"If God is looking for faithful stewards, then it may be generally assumed that when He finds them He will desire to trust them with more. But, true as these blessings in kind are, the primary benefits of faithfulness in stewardship are spiritual."[4]

— SIMON WEBLEY

ASK YOURSELF: a. In what way do I need to change my attitude toward sharing my money or material possessions? b. Do I need to change my plans for how much I give and to whom?

"I place no value on anything I have or may possess except in relation to the kingdom of Christ. If anything will advance the interests of the kingdom, it shall be given away or kept, only as by giving or keeping it shall most promote the glory of Him to whom I owe all my hopes in time and eternity."

— DAVID LIVINGSTONE[*]

Stop, Think, and Pray

Look over your answers to the questions in this lesson. Pray that God will show you the things He wants you to do. Summarize what you have learned and your plan for putting it into practice.

Main lesson learned

What I am going to do

Suggested memory verse about money and materialism

Then he said to them, "Watch out! Be on your guard against all kinds of greed; a man's life does not consist in the abundance of his possessions." (Luke 12:15)

NOTES: 1. James Broad, "Christian Lifestyle," *British Navigator Log*, Summer 1977, page 7.

2. Donald Hay, *A Christian Critique of Capitalism* (Nottingham, England: Grove Books, 1982), pages 20-21.

3. *An Evangelical Commitment to a Simple Lifestyle* (Wheaton, Illinois: Lausanne Committee for World Evangelization, 1980), page 18.

4. Simon Webley, *Money Matters* (Leicester, England: InterVarsity Press, 1978), page 16.

Memorizing Scripture

As You Start to Memorize a Verse

1. Read in your Bible the context of each verse you memorize.
2. Try to gain a clear understanding of what each verse actually means. (You may want to read the verse in other Bible translations or paraphrases to get a better grasp of the meaning.)
3. Read the verse several times thoughtfully, aloud or in a whisper. This will help you grasp the verse as a whole. Each time you read it, say the topic, reference, verse, and then the reference again.
4. Discuss the verse with God in prayer, and continue to seek His help for success in Scripture memory.

While You Are Memorizing a Verse

5. Work on saying the verse aloud as much as possible.
6. Learn the topic and reference first.
7. After learning the topic and reference, learn the first phrase of the verse. Once you have learned the topic, reference, and first phrase and have repeated them several times, continue adding more phrases, one at a time.
8. Think about how the verse applies to you and your daily circumstances.
9. Always include the topic and reference as part of the verse as you learn it and review it.

After You Have Memorized a Verse

10. Write the verse from memory and check your accuracy. This deepens the impression in your mind.
11. Review the verse immediately after learning it, and repeat it frequently in the next few days. This is crucial for getting the verse firmly fixed in your mind, because of how quickly we tend to forget what we have recently learned.
12. REVIEW! REVIEW! REVIEW! Repetition is the best way to engrave the verse on your memory.

Who's Who

Below, listed in alphabetical order, are biographical sketches of figures from Church history who are quoted in this book.

Augustine of Hippo (354-430)
The son of a pagan father and Christian mother, he was born and educated in North Africa. Following a dissolute lifestyle, he moved to Italy and became professor of logic in Milan. There, in 386, he was converted to Christianity. Returning to North Africa, he became Bishop of Hippo and one of the great writers and theologians of the Western Church.

Erasmus, Desiderius (1466-1536)
Dutch scholar, famous for his Greek New Testament. He spoke of the need for Church reform, although he did not identify with Luther.

Livingstone, David (1813-1873)
Scottish missionary and explorer. He established mission stations in remote parts of South Africa and discovered such natural wonders as the Victoria Falls. He was also concerned about eradicating slave trading.

Maximus Confessor (580-662)
Born in Constantinople, he was one of the most prolific writers of the Greek church. He was a monk and a defender of the

orthodox faith against the Monethelite heresy. He died from injuries received during the persecution, but his stand helped orthodoxy to triumph.

Tertullian (160-about 220)
A Roman lawyer, he was converted in mid life. He lived and worked in North Africa and became the first theologian to write in Latin. He was a brilliant writer, especially in defending Christianity against opponents. Later he joined the Montanist movement.

Wesley, John (1703-1791)
A great preacher of the English evangelical revival. Although already a Church of England minister, he came to a living faith in 1738. Prevented from speaking in churches, he traveled some two hundred fifty thousand miles and preached some forty thousand sermons, mainly in the open air. He organized the converts into classes and societies, which developed into the Methodist Church after his death.

For Further Reading

Lessons 1-6
Deuteronomy, a LIFECHANGE Bible study, NavPress.

1. Work and Rest
Peabody, Larry, *Secular Work*, Christian Literature Crusade
White, Jerry and Mary, *Your Job: Survival or Satisfaction*,
Zondervan Publishing House

2. Parents and Children
Campbell, Ross, *How to Really Love Your Child*, Victor
Books/Scripture Press
Dobson, James, *Dare to Discipline*, Tyndale House Publishers
God's Design for the Family, a Navigator Bible study series,
NavPress
Schaeffer, Edith, *What Is a Family?*, Fleming H. Revell

3. Life and Love
Schaeffer, Francis, and Koop, C. Everett, *Whatever
Happened to the Human Race?*, Good News
Publishers
Verwer, George, *Revolution of Love and Balance*, STL Books
White, Jim, *Christlikeness*, NavPress (booklet)

4. Man and Woman
Evans, Mary, *Women in the Bible*, Attic Press, Inc.

Hurley, James B., *Man and Woman in Biblical Perspective*, Zondervan Publishing House

Karssen, Gien, *Getting the Most Out of Being Single*, NavPress

Mayhall, Jack and Carole, *Marriage Takes More than Love*, NavPress

Wheat, Ed, *Love Life for Every Married Couple*, Zondervan Publishing House

White, John W., *Eros Defiled: The Christian and Sexual Sin*, InterVarsity Press

5. Honesty and Integrity

Sanchez, George, *Changing Your Thought Patterns*, NavPress (booklet)

6. Money and Materialism

Sider, Ronald S., *Rich Christians in an Age of Hunger*, Paulist Press